EMPATHY

The ability to understand another person,
and its positive effects on affective
and social relationships

Mary Casie

Table of Contents

"A man should not strive to eliminate his complexes, but to get into accord with them; they are legitimately what directs hi conduct in the world."

Sigmund Freud

INTRODUCTION

A simple definition of empathy: the ability to understand another person's feelings or experiences, by being able to put yourself in that person's situation.

According to Daniel Goleman, author of the book Emotional Intelligence, empathy is basically the ability to understand the emotions of others. He also notes that at a deeper level, it is about defining, understanding, and reacting to the concerns and needs that lie behind the emotional responses and reactions of others.

Several studies, lead one to believe that empathy is a skill that can be developed, and as with most interpersonal skills, empathy comes naturally to most people.

Signs that Betray the Absence of Empathy

1. Concentration on Oneself

A feature that peoples with an absence of empathy usually have in common, especially those who have autistic traits, is the feeling that they are focused on their inner world and are not fully aware of them.

2. Egocentrism

Something familiar in all people with a lack of empathy is self-centeredness: they see everything from their perspective, being the only one valid and not considering others' validity. There may also be selfishness: the only thing or the most important thing is what you want, the defense of your rights, and the achievement of your goals.

Thus, they can set aside pragmatic aspects of the language and send excellent hard messages without any tact towards their transmitters. This sign may not be evident in manipulation attempts if the person has great intelligence and can know cognitively how things affect others.

3. Impatience

Another common feature in non-empathic people is impatience with others: they cannot understand or value others' needs and find it irritating to have to repeat or invest time in doing things with others, integrating them.

4. Stereotypes and Prejudices Follow

Not having the capacity for empathy makes it familiar for these people to use stereotypes and prejudices, act on a cognitive level, and use labels to guide their behavior and thinking. They are also unable to see how they affect the behavior of others.

5. Aggression and Violence

Although not all people who do not have empathy develop violent attitudes (for example, people with autism have problems with compassion and are not usually violent), the truth is that not having understanding makes it easier to resort to solution styles. Aggressive or even damaging problems when there is no awareness of what this implies for the other or the suffering they can cause.

6. Lack of Regrets

Doing something that hurts others usually causes some regret in most people. However, in those who lack empathy, regrets are nonexistent or much less than usual, although they may apologize if they have the cognition that others have suffered or if it suits them for their purposes.

How Does Lack of Empathy Affect Us?

The lack of empathy in the couple is a situation that strongly affects the coexistence of the same, taking into account that heart refers to the ability of people to place themselves in the place of the other and feel their suffering in a real way. That is to say, and if you are empathetic, you can feel the pain of other people as yours and sympathize with them.

In love relationships, this factor is essential for the couple to overcome the adversities of emotional coexistence.

When there is a lack of significant empathy within the love bond, the relationship becomes dysfunctional, proving damaging for both members.

On the one hand, the person who does not receive empathy is in a situation of vulnerability; since he is alone regardless of whether the other person is with him in terms of the relationship (technically), there is no real accompaniment emotionally neither affective.

On the other hand, the couple who does not provide empathy is placed in inflicting emotional pain, even if he does nothing to offend or mistreat the other intentionally; lack of emotionality results in damage.

In relationships, the members must be emotionally linked so that the other's sadness becomes the sadness of both, and based on that emotional connection. You can reach the best solutions together.

But when this empathic bond does not exist on one or both parties, the relationship wears out. When there is no empathy, some relationships can last for some time but usually end up on bad terms.

How to Overcome This Situation in the Couple?

1. Value the Opinions of Your Partner

The empathy link begins to be cultivated from mutual respect; a first step may be to consider our partner's opinions. Not only hear them answer you, but actively listen to what you have to tell us.

2. Avoid Value Judgments

A fairly common mistake in relationships is usually the value judgments issued on one of the members' whim, without having any sustenance. This kind of unjustified opinions only manages to move the other further away and generate distrust in the relationship; they should be avoided.

3. Cultivate Patience

A virtue that must prevail in relationships, especially in difficult moments, is patience. This ability to withstand the impulses to act or say things simultaneously leads us towards empathic behavior towards the other, facilitating communication; we must encourage tolerance.

4. Promotes Understanding

We should comprehend that we will not always be right and that sometimes it is good to give our arm to twist when we are wrong. It is essential to achieve compression in relationships, to be able to see things as they are happening and not as we would like them to be.

5. Practice Kindness

A relationship should be based on mutual respect and kindness in the members of the emotional bond. Regardless of the jokes that may exist in the relationship, affectionate treatment should always prevail in couple dynamics. This point is indispensable to achieve empathy.

6. Take Care of the Way You Express Yourself

It is not the same to participate in a kind and calm way than by shouting and insults. This aspect is also part of the kindness of the couple, but based on powerful speech. It is not enough to say things, but you also have to know how to tell them.

7. Make Peace a Goal

Regardless of the conflict that arises, try to visualize a possible outcome where both end up in healthy peace, both at the level of the relationship and at the individual level. If you make peace a goal within your relationship, eventually, you will solve the problems adequately and constructively.

8. Bet on Honesty

Sometimes the lack of empathy can be caused by the absence of affection for the other person; sometimes, there are cases where couples maintain a relationship based solely on the habit of being together.

How to Develop Your Empathy?

Experience the Main Differences Between People

Individuals with little or no empathy skills may have an intellectual awareness of these differences. However, until they experience these differences, their empathic skills are likely to remain relatively limited.

Learn to Identify Your Feelings - Develop Some Emotional Intelligence

Many of us are so "objective" and "controlled" about feelings that we cannot quickly identify them in ourselves, let alone in others.

For example, we may confuse analytical ideas and rational thoughts with irrational ones. When someone tells you how you feel about a job, you can answer pragmatically, "I think we have a lot to do." Instead of thinking about how you feel from your feelings, emotions, desires, and frustrations about the project. Or we may be unable to distinguish between related (similar) emotions, for example, differentiating frustration from irritability or happiness from excitement. It is a real problem that must be dealt with by daily debugging exercises and a fundamental understanding of our emotions and the emotions of others.

Silently compare your answers to what you might have thought they would be. This approach helps you hone your empathic skills and enables you to learn more about your employees.

They will talk to the person sitting next to her on the bus. They maintain the genuine interest we all had as children. They find other people more attractive than themselves. Still, they don't want to question them, respecting the advice of oral historian Studs Terkel: "Don't is an examiner, be the interested researcher."

How Important is Empathy in Our Lives?

•Solidarity: It is wrong to think that this word is directly linked only to volunteer work. Looking at others, understanding your difficulties, and offering help when you need it and when you can, is a valuable way to show solidarity. So do not close your eyes to your friends, family, and co-workers who need your help for some reason.

•Respect: Understanding that each one chooses their path to life and respecting this decision is fundamental for any human being. Unfortunately, this is not what continually happens globally, but it is not because you will not act politely and kindly to anyone. Respect the lifestyle choices, religion, sexual orientation, political opinion, and so many other topics that can cause conversation problems. If older people didn't question what is different about them, the world would be living more harmoniously today.

14

•Listen to the essence: Coaching teaches how important it is to listen to people in nature. It means that you listen to what the other has to say, assimilate, accept, and respectfully give your opinion. This kind of behavior demonstrates that you are concerned about getting everyone's views expressed in due space. This behavior is essential for a healthy debate.

•Learning: You must continuously be evolving throughout your life. For this, you mustn't stop studying. Sharing knowledge with other professionals, healthily discussing, reading, researching, and pursuing complementary courses and coaching are all ways to keep you updated and evolve regularly. So never forget to invest in your continuing education and different ways of learning.

•Collectivity: Collective awareness is fundamental in business environments and outside them, as this is essential for a good coexistence in society. Much more than just knowing how to work in groups, the community teaches to respect each other's opinions and to include everyone, even those who have had fewer opportunities.

Types of Empathy

Empathy is generally the ability to sense other people's emotions and conditions from their perspective without inclining on your understanding. The heart gives you the ability to imagine what someone else is thinking about something. Pro-social behavior emanates from within someone without any external influence from another person as a result of empathy. Empathy makes you behave more compassionately.

Empathic accuracy is a higher level of empathy where you understand how someone else feels and discern their thoughts and actions. You can further adjust your actions and reactions based on this understanding. The ability to mimic another's emotions without being able to sense them outlasts childhood development and continues into adulthood, suggesting that it can be developed further with practice and experience.

Cognitive Empathy

Walk a mile in someone else's shoes, and you understand them is an old saying that seems to encompass the meaning of empathy to many people, but that is cognitive empathy. Being cognitive is thinking or knowing. Cognition is when you evaluate, analyze, and understand what your partner is going through to identify with the situation through your knowledge. You can call this a type of empathy because you can place the problem probably because you have been in a similar situation before.

Emotional Empathy

When you can feel what someone else is feeling yet, you have never experienced the same, but you have knowledge about it, that is when you say you are experiencing emotional empathy. When you hear of a particular pain, then you identify with that pain because you have probably seen someone else in a similar situation is emotional contagion. The mirror neurons are what controls emotional empathy. You mirror what you see in another person and start imagining it might happen to you, and then you feel compassion.

Compassionate Empathy

Compassionate empathy is similar to the critical word of compassion. When you feel compassionate about someone or something, you get a concern that takes you to the next level of intending to mitigate the problem. Human empathy is the best form of heart. When your spouse is seeking compassion, he or she is not just seeking cognitive empathy or a need for you to feel their pain, get emotional, and burst into tears (the emotional heart). What your spouse is seeking is to satisfy his or her understanding need. Sympathize with your spouse and take crucial action to help your spouse resolve the issue.

Importance of Empathy in a Relationship

Having fights between couples is not unique; some get to an extent where they cannot see eye to eye. Disagreements may occur because of significant family decisions like how many kids to have. To more straightforward issues like where to live and the simplest like what to have for dinner. It will help if you put yourself into your partner's shoes when you get to such times. Try to reason from his or her perspective and see if it makes sense to you too. It is useful to deliberate and finalize the issue without dividing the plan of intention; let your focus be on bridging the divide and getting past your differences.

Empathy is one trait that genuinely helps you to learn how to give your mate maximum attention. Learning to empathize with your spouse allows you to shower him with the right amounts of attention and love.

Compassion is something that is put into practice. When you can see the world from someone's eyes, it provides you with an excellent opportunity to be a compassionate person. A good example is when your mate is working in a company. According to their profession, they face different challenges and pressures. Once you can see things from her perspective, it gives you an understanding of how she does her things the way she does them or why your mate is the way they are. As a spouse, you try to make the world a better place for them with such a clear understanding because you care and are compassionate. When your spouse is happy and comfortable, it is almost palpable that you also be happy and satisfied.

Through empathy, it is undeniable to develop patience. At times you might overreact to something and lose your temper just because you see things the wrong way. Empathy helps you to choose your battles wisely because not everything needs your reaction.

How to Nature Empathy

Empathy is like a force that works to maintain order and cooperation when people are working together. It is a precursor for intimacy, trust, and belonging because it allows you to understand and relate to your spouse well. Empathy creates a feeling of guilt when you turn a blind eye to an unhealthy situation that your partner is going through. Compassion benefits the other person and you as an individual; it creates an experience of joy and happiness. When empathy is out of kindness, it increases cooperation, forgiveness, strengthens relationships, decreases aggression, and judgment hence improving mental and physical health. When you are happy, you tend to be less aware of the negative emotions in other people who rate themselves as more empathetic.

Prioritize Listening

Empathy only begins when you set within you the intention to listen for emotions. If you want to connect with what someone else is feeling, you must recognize or know what the feeling they have is. To be able to identify your partner's emotions, you need to listen with excellent attention. Keenness in listening should have nothing to do with establishing a defense for yourself while talking, but establishing how to help them. It is possible to have a conversation and concentrate on your feelings, trying to find out how you can communicate them to your partner, hence not giving attention to what is going on with your companion. Imagine a situation where a friend calls you to tell you they have had a break-up and it is not easy for them; if this person is your true friend, you can easily recognize the emotions from their voice without having to see them, and you can give the relevant empathy measures.

Share Feelings

Sharing feelings is equal to putting yourself in your spouse's shoes, which helps you recognize your partner's emotions. You might be confusing empathy for feeling what you would think if you are in that situation. Still, in the real sense, the heart is merely stepping aside and adopting your companions' emotions for a few moments.

Actively Asking Questions

When you are having a conversation, and you are keen to ask questions, it does not only show you are concentrating, but it allows you to be more attuned to your partner's emotions. When you get the attuning to your partner's feelings, the result is you can notice when they are down or hurt even before they tell you about it. You can ask your partner about their emotional state, and this helps to show both of you that you are investing in their happiness and relationship. You can even ask without expecting any detailed answers, but just to let your spouse know, I am interested to know.

Withhold Judgment

Both of you must appreciate the fact that there is no reward in judging someone. When in a relationship or marriage, your focus should be on growing and teaching each other together. You should try your best to help each other when the need is yet without being judgmental of the other person and making your partner feel small. When you know the person you are working with will not judge you, it allows you to be free and willing to share the details of your situation regardless of whether it leads to success or not.

Consider Needs and Wants

When you have empathy or merely the ability to take things and look at them beyond your perspective and incline to that of your partner, you find you have an easy time in decision making. It happens to be so because you allow room for meaningful consideration of your partner's needs and wants before making a decision or acting.

Be Self-Compassionate

Empathy begins with you; it is difficult you be empathetic with someone else, yet you do not empathize with yourself. Self-compassion is all about treating yourself with kindness, care, and understanding. You can always practice this skill when you notice and acknowledge that you are having a hard time without trying to catastrophize the situation. At this time, you can check yourself and know what you need, which you can even make a list of the healthy strategies you can use.

Impact of Lack of Empathy on Relationships

What ends a relationship is the small little things and not the big things which only point out that there was no serious relationship in the first place. Think of empathy as basically being observant. Let your spouse penetrate your five senses or any other sense you might be having, which goes beyond a loved one just communicating their needs. You must stay aware of someone else other than yourself if you intend to maintain long-lasting relationships. With a lack of empathy, you are merely creating openings for;

●Lack of respect – when you can see your companion fully as a realized person rather than a convenient extension of your needs; that is empathy. It is essential to be willing to speak the unspoken language in a relationship. Let your partner know that they are real, and whatever they are experiencing is expected, which raises respect both ways.

●Lack of appreciation – when you lack empathy, it is so easy to lack appreciation too. You come back home, and your clothes are well cleaned, ironed, and arranged, your dinner is ready, and the house is sparkling clean, yet your loved one has to study still. You cannot see and feel how much someone has put in for all this to do all these, then what you are doing is reducing their actions to expectations that do not deserve an appreciation.

●Lack of reciprocation – people have different degrees of generosity, but no matter how generous you might be, as a human being, you often expect exchange. You might want to confuse reciprocation with tit for tat or revenge or keeping a scorecard, but that is not it. Your lover can give you a great foot rub bath, which in return you can make for them their favorite salad or ice cream or coffee, and all these are actions of reciprocation. Reciprocating does not look at how much time or energy you put in it so that your lover can put in the same amount of energy or time, but it is simple to sign off. I appreciate

•Lack of connection – empathy allows a good relationship with your loved one. There is something so beautiful about a couple that attunes to the flow of one another. The couple moves, think, behave, and anticipate in a particularly admirable way. Connection happens because the couple is open to one another, they understand each other's moods, they enjoy each other's company. They seem bonded beyond the surface roles, all because of empathy.

•

How to Exercise Empathy in Times of Crisis

Conflict is an inevitable part of any relationship, especially when you spend a lot of time together and rely on each other for many things. Learning to deal with conflict effectively can ensure that you can overcome it by having the right tools on hand anytime an argument arises in your marriage. If you are not effectively managing disagreements and conflicts, these smaller arguments can fester and turn into larger disputes over time. As a result, it can drive a massive wedge between you and your partner.

Knowing how to handle conflicts and conflict resolution in a marriage is a tricky task, as both of you will likely need to break many bad habits and learn how to communicate more effectively. It can take time and practice, so make sure that you are patient with your partner and trusting in the process. The more considerate you are of each other, the easier it will be for you to begin integrating these new techniques into your conflicts and experiencing fewer arguments and resentment and more resolutions and forgiveness.

Avoid Turning Disagreements into Fights

One intense way to handle disagreements in your marriage is to avoid letting disagreements turn into fights. Conflicts generally occur before an actual fight officially starts, and learning how to recognize these disagreements can support you and your spouse in stopping them from turning into something bigger. Inputting your conflict resolution skills into the conversation when the controversy starts can prevent it from spiraling.

When you can avoid having arguments turn into fights, it is easier to handle resolutions. The only thing that needs to be accomplished is finding a solution that both of you can agree on. However, if it turns into a fight, it might result in you also having to heal from hurt feelings and resentment.

Make Sure You Fight Fairly

If a disagreement does escalate into a fight, you must fight fairly. Fighting dirty can result in hurt feelings, pain, and resentment. As a result, it is much harder to come back from. If you do find yourself fighting, refrain from pointing blame, calling names, attacking someone based on their past experiences, or using parts of someone's life against them. Trying to bully your partner to see that you are right or hurt them because you feel that they hurt you is not okay. In doing so, you can quickly destroy the trust and intimacy in your marriage and find yourselves feeling resentful toward each other and unwilling to come together to find a solution. It is not a healthy state to be in as it can result in no solution being seen, or worse, it can result in your marriage ending.

When you are fighting, always make sure that you fight clean. Use compassion when fighting, do not get sarcastic, do not fight with contempt, and not call your partner names. Doing so can result in you becoming a bully and can be taken as a sign of abuse. Abuse at any point, even if it is unintentional during a heated fight, can be painful and difficult to heal. If it happens multiple times, it can result in significant damage and a lot that both partners need to heal.

Apologize When You Do Something Wrong

Never wait for your partner to ask for an apology. Instead, if you have done something wrong, admit fault and apologize for what you did. Not apologizing when you have done something wrong suggests that you do not care that you hurt your partner's feelings or do not take responsibility for your actions. Both can result in your partner feeling like nothing will ever change and that you will both continue to have a poor relationship from now on. As a result, they may lose hope.

If your partner claims you have done something and you do not recall doing it, you may struggle to apologize because you might feel like you do not want to take the blame for something you do not think you have done. You should apologize anyway. Apologize for the fact that your partner feels as though you have hurt their feelings. Then, ask them to elaborate on how you hurt their feelings and what you can do to avoid hurting their feelings again in the future. It shows that even though you might not understand right now, you are willing to try and that you want to make things right and treat them better in the future.

Take a Timeout If You Need To

During an argument, it is not unreasonable to ask for a timeout. When things get heated, and feelings are being hurt, or your arguing is not productive, taking a timeout is a great way to relax, ground yourself, and remember the goal. Generally, the goal is for each partner to feel heard and understood and for a mutual agreement to be reached so that you can overcome the argument with a resolution.

If your argument has gotten to the point where no resolution is being considered or reached, where you feel like you are not making any progress, where feelings are being hurt, or where it feels like it is becoming too much, call a timeout. Take some time away from each other and breathe so that you can let your emotions filter out, and you can both come back into a clear-thinking space.

Make an agreement that you agree to calm down and come back to find a resolution upon calling for a timeout. You should also make sure that you both set a time. That way, both of you have clear expectations of when the other will be ready to talk again, and no one feels as though they are being pressured to speak sooner than they are prepared to, or like they are waiting indefinitely for the other partner to be ready.

Articulate the Real Reason You Are Frustrated

During a disagreement, you must take the time to articulate the real reason as to why you are frustrated or upset. It is not enough to know that your partner knows precisely what has caused your bitter feelings. It would be better if you took the time to explain why you are upset, what they did that contributed to it, and how you feel it can be resolved. It gives your partner a clear understanding as to what is being addressed in the conversation.

When you do not take the time to outline what you are upset about, your partner is left guessing. They may think that you are upset about something other than what has upset you. Then, they may be arguing in one direction about one topic while you say in another order about a different matter. Furthermore, it can lead to you both feeling as if you are not being understood. It can be frustrating because you feel as though you are explaining yourself well, but your partner may think that you are referencing something different from what you are. As a result, it can lead to more hurt feelings and more profound arguments.

Being clear on what has caused your frustrations ensures that your partner knows precisely what you are upset about. That way, they can address that exact topic rather than addressing something that is not related to your frustrations. It keeps you both focused on the same subject and working toward a solution.

Take Responsibility for Your Feelings and Opinions

During an argument, you must take responsibility for your feelings and opinions. Always use "I" statements to show that you are your thoughts and feelings rather than passing blame on your partner. Even if you say something, say it to share that you are talking about your perspective of what they said and not what they meant. That way, if what you perceived and what they meant were two completely different things, it does not seem like you are feeding words into their mouth.

Furthermore, make sure that you are not considering your feelings and opinions to be absolute truths. Instead, they are yours. It means that you take the time to acknowledge that many different ideas, thoughts, feelings, and perceptions can be considered authentic. When

28

you take responsibility in this way and keep an open mind, you ensure that you are validating your partner, too. You do not want to get into an argument over who is right and who is wrong because chances are both of you are right in your ways. Knowing how to recognize this and respect it ensures that you stay focused on the real issue and not a power struggle.

We live in troubled times. The divisions are clear, the future is uncertain, and tensions are high. This week has been hard for many of us, and you may have realized that it's tough to consider the other side of what we see — that is, to put ourselves in the shoes of people who believe differently from us. But empathy isn't just sympathy or pity; it's a powerful tool for finding common ground when things seem hopeless.

So, if you're looking to understand your fellow citizens better and practice empathy this week - there are good ways to get started:

Spend time talking with people who have different political views from yours. One of the core aspects of empathy is being able to see things from a different perspective. To practice that, start by talking with people who have different political views from yours. Ask them why they think differently than you do, and sit with their answers. Even if you disagree, they'll help you understand how others think, and that will help build your empathy muscles for what comes next.

Commit to learning new information about issues that are important to people who disagree with you. Often disagreements stem from a lack of understanding, so opening up your mind to learn about those issues can feel like a big step toward understanding the other side better. It is a great way to empathize with the other side - listen first and then consider talking.

Be curious about other people. One way to open your mind up to others is by opening your curiosity up to them. To do that, ask questions of people you know and trust that might challenge you or help you see things differently. Challenge yourself to be curious about their lives and their views without judging them or changing them. The more interested you are, the more empathy you'll practice with every encounter.

Remember that it's okay not to understand all of someone's story right away. Often when you're empathetic, you'll be told things that don't seem to make sense at first. You'll need to work hard to push through those moments of confusion and keep trying to understand how someone else sees the world. It takes practice, but it's worth it because the more you can understand another person's perspective and their story, the more empathy you'll have for them and all people.

Find common ground wherever possible. Whether it's talking about your families or interests, finding shared values can help build empathy over time. As long as you're respectful of people and their views, find common ground with them whenever possible and offer gratitude for those connections.

Relationship between Emotional Intelligence and Empathy

Empathy has been linked with emotional intelligence. But how does one develop the other? And which is more important for professionals?

Emotional intelligence is the ability to identify and understand emotions in oneself and others and use dynamic information to guide thinking and behaviors. Emotional Intelligence and Empathy

It is often thought that emotional intelligence is the capacity to identify, understand and manage emotions in oneself and others. Empathy can be defined as the ability to share another person's emotions or feelings, including understanding what they are thinking or feeling.

The two concepts are closely related because of their similar focus on emotion regulation strategies such as awareness of one's own feelings and recognition of others' emotions. Research has found that empathetic people generally have higher levels of emotional intelligence (Rosenbaum). Similarly, people with high levels of emotional intelligence are naturally more compassionate.

The term "emotional intelligence" first appeared in a publication by psychologist Peter Salovey and his colleagues in 1990. The researchers believed that emotional intelligence is a type of social intelligence on which human interaction and personal development largely depend. In the same article, Salovey and Mayer suggest that this social or emotional "intelligence" is an ability to reason about emotions, regulate one's feelings, and motivate oneself.

Daniel Goleman is a psychologist and author of several popular articles on emotional intelligence. According to Goleman, an individual's level of emotional intelligence is determined by his ability to regulate emotions, handle relationships, make the right decisions and maintain high motivation. Emotional intelligence is not limited to individuals; it can also be applied to teams or companies. As a whole, each group has its level of emotional intelligence that determines how well it functions as a whole. Goleman also states that one's emotional intelligence level can be boosted through specific techniques involving visualization and cognitive behavioral therapy.

Evidence shows that people with high levels of Emotional intelligence tend to be more empathetic than those with lower emotional intelligence levels. The heart is an essential social skill in communication. In the field of psychology, it is defined as "the ability to share and understand another person's experience and emotions." It has two components: cognitive empathy, which refers to understanding others' emotions; and affective empathy, which refers to feeling what others might be feeling or experiencing similar feelings.

Management expert Peter Drucker describes empathy as "knowing what other people are thinking without them having to tell you. It is an essential quality for salespeople to have." Indeed, empathy plays an essential role in the field of management. It can be used to motivate employees and establish trust. With trust comes commitment, respect, and positive interactions within the workplace. Companies with positive work environments pay close attention to their employees' welfare and seek to engage them fully at all levels, promoting full emotional engagement with the business strategy and shared objectives.

Emotional intelligence experts argue that emotional intelligence is crucial to ineffective communication. "The ability to empathize is ineffective central management," says Daniel Goleman. "Managers who can put themselves in another's shoes are more successful than those who can't. They can anticipate and handle problems before they blow up into full-blown crises." Emotional intelligence also helps managers to take criticism and direction from their superiors in a positive way.

Salovey and Mayer's article on emotional intelligence has been one of the most cited papers in psychology. They have developed a model which describes emotional intelligence as including four aspects: perceiving emotion, using emotions to facilitate thought, understanding emotions, motivation and affect, and managing emotions. The authors suggest that this way of understanding emotional intelligence helps explain a wide range of social behaviors.

It's vital for leaders in all fields, including business, education, politics, law enforcement, the military (to mention a few), because it guides how they make decisions. Successful leaders are empathetic—they can see when someone is crying or happy or angry. They are in tune with other people's emotions. They can sense when something is wrong, and they can respond to it appropriately or have the ability to see from someone else's perspective.

Empathy is useful when leaders are trying to motivate their employees and colleagues or when they are trying to understand a particular situation. As a leader, you must motivate and inspire your staff — give them reasons to feel good about what they do. You must also motivate yourself—keep your morale high and continue doing what you must do for things to work out. You must also have the ability, as a leader, to put yourself in someone else's shoes. You must have the ability to show compassion and communicate with your peers and colleagues in a way that makes them feel comfortable and able to trust you. If you can do these things, then you will be more effective as a leader.

Empathy is helpful, but it's easy for leaders to take it too far and "walk in another person's shoes" too much. A leader must have the ability to take a distance and think clearly about what needs to be done. You must understand what you are feeling and why you feel the way you do, but keep in mind that it's OK to put yourself in another person's shoes when it is useful, but not when it will hinder your ability to make the right decisions.

As a leader in any field, you need to know how your actions affect other people. It means that you occasionally have to do things that may seem unfair or inappropriate. It's essential for leaders to know how they affect others — they should know how people feel about what they do.

You cannot know if you are a good leader by reading this article. There is no one else who can tell you if you are a good leader. The only way to know for sure if you have what it takes to be a great leader is by trying and seeing what happens.

There are specific characteristics that all influential leaders have, regardless of the field in which they work:

As a leader, it is crucial for your employees to feel comfortable and confident with your decisions and what you ask them to do. There are times when you will ask them to do things that they aren't sure about or don't want to do, but if they trust and respect you, then the chances are good that they will do it. On the other hand, if your employees don't respect or trust you, then chances are good that they won't do it. Furthermore, if your employees don't feel comfortable around you or feel ignored by you, then they won't have the ability to trust or respect you.

Communication is vital to leadership success. Great leaders can speak and listen effectively — they use words to motivate other people to follow their lead. Great leaders also listen to what others have to say. They don't feel threatened by input from others — they want to hear what their employees have to say because they need to understand all sides of every situation. Great leaders can motivate their employees — they can get them excited about doing specific things that, on the surface, may not seem exciting or fun.

If you are a leader and desire your employees and colleagues to care about what you do and how you do it, you must be able to care about them.

Emotional intelligence positively increases your self-motivated ability, which leads to living a better life and growing your career more quickly: the self-awareness and emotional skills of people who have high EQ shine cheerful sunshine on their motor skills. Sometimes, when we've had little motivation for a long draw, it's hard to get motivated again, kind of like taking a cheat day that turns into a cheat week. We are merely human, so this is natural for us. We want more than we can quickly get, but we don't feel motivated to try hard to get what we want.

Motivated people set goals, and whenever they find themselves in crisis, they wonder why this is. Maybe the things happening in your life right now are making you too busy even to think you are positive. Or perhaps you don't get enough sleep. Either way, you can get out of that crisis. Setting a goal and achieving it is excellent. Plans help us focus our attention on the most important things, such as the ultimate goal. It's also easier to know for sure what you want when you focus on a single goal. Freelance motivation is pretty tricky, so make it easier by becoming a goal setter and a go-getter!

Motivated people also seek inspiration. One of the most significant impulses for anyone is something that truly inspires them deep inside. Look for someone who can be a good role model or idol and listen to the words they say. You can often find motivational speeches and inspiring stories easily on video streaming services. Emotional intelligence helps us get inspired because people with higher EQs are more profound thinkers. They can appreciate the beauty of things that others may not always see. You can find inspiration everywhere if you look for it and sincerely hope to find it. It's an incredibly positive trait to have to be able to locate inspiration wherever you are.

Be enthusiastic about achieving your goal. Do your best to feel and show enthusiasm. If someone tells you that they don't feel it or don't trust the process anymore, ask them to keep moving forward and be confident. As already mentioned, finding your inspiration can be the thrust inside you that makes you excited to get up every day and start on the coffee machine; excitement is a powerful emotion that makes us do things we never thought humanly possible. Because it makes our blood pump and our adrenaline flows through our bodies.

As you interact with people from all walks of life, certain traits will tell you that you are working with a compassionate individual. Common personality attributes that will be evident in an empathic individual are briefly talked about.

Characteristics of Authentic Empathy

Empathy is defined as the ability to share somebody else's feelings, emotions, and experiences. It is a robust human quality that demonstrates compassion. Some of the common symptoms of struggling with empathy are poor communication skills, judged by others for being inconsiderate or self-absorbed in interactions with others. The heart requires a certain degree of emotional intelligence - the ability to recognize and identify one's own emotions and those of other people - because it means understanding what someone else might be going through when they have feelings that may not be apparent at first.

Empathy cannot be faked since it takes an insightful human being to identify genuine emotions. A person may appear to be empathic but might possess self-serving or manipulative motives. It is essential for people to continually evaluate their behavior to become better at recognizing the difference between genuine and phony empathy.

When it comes to authentic empathy, a recent study has invented a new way of gauging its characteristics and proposed a psychological scale for evaluating the likelihood that a person might possess such ability. It is a new approach to determine the extent to which someone might be capable of demonstrating authentic empathy. This scale will help people evaluate the level of empathy they show to others and improve their potential for leading more effort in the process.

Highly Sensitive

Guys with empathy will be compassionate. These are the type of individuals who will be there for you no matter what happens. They have a substantial background of what emotions you are working through. They can put themselves in your shoes. Unfortunately, the world is not so friendly, and therefore, such people often get easily hurt.

Highly Intuitive

Empathic people will want to face the world with the help of their intuition. Before taking any actions, they will want to follow their guts. The exciting thing about this is that they approach life confidently. At times, this helps them enter into blissful relationships simply because they believed in their intuitions.

They Give too Much

They are compassionate means that you can understand the emotions of other people. Therefore, a common trait of empathic individuals is that they love to give. Their act of giving is what drives them to help others out of their misery.

Need for Solitude

At times empathic people will be misunderstood due to their desire to be left alone. Their constant need for solitude is meant to help them connect with their inner selves. Eventually, this is what makes them self-aware of their emotions before understanding the feelings of others.

Improving Your Empathy

Considering the desirable traits of tenderhearted individuals, there are various ways in which you can learn to improve your empathy.

Get Feedback

Sometimes you need to ask other people about your social relations. Don't just assume that because people are smiling at you, they are happy. Get honest feedback from your friends and romantic partners. They will help you identify areas where you need to improve.

Listen

Active listening can also play a big part in enhancing your empathy. Through listening, you get to understand people better and reason out with them.

Smile at People

Never overlook the power of smiling at people. A keen eye should tell you that smiling is contagious. Science tells us that smiling liberates chemicals in the brain, which helps you maintain a good mood. As such, the act of smiling will not only help you increase your health but will also boost your empathy.

Scrutinize Your Biases

Equally, you should consider scrutinizing your biases. These are the factors that often prevent you from being compassionate with others. For instance, you might fail to connect people because you prejudice them based on their gender, age, or race. To increase your empathic levels, try to examine your biases and find a way of ignoring them. Ultimately, you will appreciate the importance of seeing people for who they are.

Challenge Yourself

It is also essential that you get out of your comfort zone to understand people better. Don't allow conversations to end abruptly; challenge yourself by bringing in creative and exciting topics that will spur real talks. Ideally, you will connect with people far beyond knowing about where they live.

How Highly Sensitive People Manage Their Emotions

Most people will attest to the fact that it is not easy to deal with emotions. It is an overwhelming task. Empathic individuals are known to be highly emotional. However, it begs to wonder how they effectively manage their emotions.

If you are a highly emotional person, it is imperative to learn how to deal with your emotions. It will confirm that your feelings do not blind you. Honestly, at times you need to wake up to reality. Before you can empathize with other people, you need to understand your boundaries.

Put Yourself First

Without a doubt, putting your needs first might sound controversial because it is an uncommon trait of compassionate people. Nonetheless, for you to successfully take care of others' needs, you need to begin by sorting your demands first. The clue here is that you should not be depleted. You should have the right energy to be able to see and help others out of their predicament.

Set Clear Boundaries

Sure, you are an empathic person. It does not mean that you can help everyone around you. You need to know that you are also human, with flaws. As such, set clear boundaries to help you know when to stop. People should even understand that you have limits.

Let it Go

Indeed, compassionate people will want to walk in the shoes of other people and give them a supporting hand to lean on in times of need. Similarly, when things are good, they will want to share moments of joy with them. In sad moments, empathic folks must learn how to let go. For instance, you might drain your energy when trying to mourn with a friend. In such cases, you need to embrace the idea of separation. There are some emotions that you need to separate yourself from. It might appear selfish, but you will also be helping yourself by managing your empathic nature in the real sense.

Listen to Your Emotions

Another essential step that empathetic people should remember to take is to listen to their emotions. You might be too focused on what others are feeling, and you could end up forgetting about yourself. For you to understand other people, you should first begin by comprehending and managing your own emotions.

Practice Celebrating

An individual who often listens and understands other people, you know what it means to feel happy. Also, you are fully aware of what someone can feel when they are in pain. Unfortunately, negative feelings will stick around for long as compared to happy feelings.

You should practice celebrating by reminding yourself of the good things you have achieved in your life. It doesn't have to be something big; honor any milestone you reach, as this will invite positive feelings your way.

Undeniably, having an empathic attribute will help you create blissful relationships with people since you can easily connect with them. However, you should not forget that you need to keep your life balanced. You need to pay attention to your feelings before committing yourself to others. First, manage your own before helping others.

Understanding the Potential of Being Empathic, Controlling Overwhelming Feelings

Besides people gaining the perception that you are too sensitive, there are numerous reasons why it is important to be empathic. Human beings can be unpredictable at times. When we watch the news and read the newspaper headlines, we often wonder how people can be so inhumane with their heinous acts. Building an empathic culture will, in the long run, help you grow your emotional intelligence. The mere fact that you can understand other people's feelings implies that you are emotionally smart.

Positive Vibe

There is a sensation that comes with knowing that you have helped other people deal with challenging situations. Being empathic will, therefore, invite positive feelings to your life. You might not be rewarded physically, but a compassionate nature always pays off.

Develop an Identity

People will always have an identity to relate to you with. If you are a cold person, they will simply know you for who you are. When in need of help, you can rest assured that most people will not want to help you. As a compassionate individual, you will develop a unique identity that tells a lot about how good you are. Again, this gives you a reason to be happy that you are making this world a better place to live.

Emotional and Physical Health

As people seek ways of keeping themselves healthy and fit, they forget that empathy is a remedy. Well, this might sound strange since the heart is all about understanding people's feelings. They were empathetic means that you could learn more about how other people behave. Therefore, it gives you an opportunity of learning from others. By paying attention to people's feelings, you can adjust accordingly and live a healthier and happier life.

Additionally, connecting with other people is an essential part of being a human being. Simply put, you have to create friends and learn how to live with them. Consequently, knowing how to interact with others effectively will keep you emotionally healthy as you can freely connect with those around you.

Lowering Stress

The virtue of being empathetic will also benefit you by helping you deal with stress. Bearing in mind that you can manage your emotions and those of others, it means you can handle stress better than other folks. You have been through challenging situations since you have tried to understand others. Therefore, there is a high likelihood that you can challenge yourself and effectively handle stressful moments.

Conflict Resolution

Conflicts will always arise. It could occur in your private life or at work. Sometimes it is difficult to deal with conflicts because our differences blind us from realizing why it is vital to compromise. An empathic person will listen and comprehend why others are angered.

They will treasure the importance of finding solutions above anything else. Consequently, through their compassionate nature, they will prevent conflicts from escalating.

Supporting Socially Desirable Values

There is no single negative social value that could be linked to empathy. The idea of being empathic promotes socially desirable values. These are individuals who want the best for the people around them. They desire to see people collaborate, understand each other, and, most importantly, heal themselves.

Accordingly, there is great potential in being empathic. Some might perceive you as emotionally weak, but in the real sense, you are more robust. You are more in tune with your emotions, and therefore, you can be recognized as an emotionally intelligent person.

The sheer fact that you can connect with others more profoundly means that you create the perfect example of being a human being— part of being compassionate means that you treasure connections over disconnection. Living and connecting with people is what defines us as human beings. Without the associations we have made to this point, we wouldn't have been where we are.

Typical Behavior of Authentic Empathetic People

Empathy is often described as "putting oneself in another person's shoes," meaning to think about the experiences others have had from their point of view. While this is accurate, there is much more to it than that. A way to describe what empathy means is understanding something even when you do not understand it at all. No people have had similar life and experiences. We have been through things that others have not, and there are things other people in our lives have been through that we have not.

Being Supportive of a Friend through a Difficult Time

When a friend is facing a crisis, it is hard to know what to do or say. You want to help but are afraid of overstepping boundaries. Do not fear giving compassion. That damages our relationships. Be present. You do not have to offer a solution to their problem. That isn't something you could do. They probably have had their fair share of experiences already with people leaving them out in the lurch. The fact that you are staying beside them and reaching out to them means you are a good friend. How do we put this into practice?

You can judge by specific nonverbal cues whether you have their interest or are losing them. If they are leaned in towards you, making eye contact, observing you, these are all signs you are on the right track. If they are not making eye contact, checking the time, and talking amongst themselves, you lose your audience's attention and need to take steps to bring their attention back to you.

It is where empathy comes in to gain your listener's interest once again. You need to connect with your audience to know what action to take next. If your audience looks offended, take a look into yourself. Is there a chance you are using this presentation to get on a soapbox? If so, it is time to create a diversion. Create a more lighthearted tone in your presentation. You also could move the discussion to a more neutral tone, making your points informative rather than opinionated.

As a caveat, some audience members will not be paying attention no matter what you do. Whether they are distracted by family problems or do not want to be here, you will not be able to get their attention. Do not take this personally.

What Can We Do to Increase Our Empathy?

Empathy is much more profound than just listening to the other side of the story. It is about putting yourself into their mindset. Truly listen to what the other person has to say and take it in. It leads to miscommunications, and we can wind up missing things that we would have tapped into. We can offer that grief is the last loving thing we can give to the ones we love. Love is the only thing that will provide comfort to those in distress. Just giving them love and letting them know that you have their support means you are giving them empathy.

Empathy means reading nonverbal cues from other people, such as facial expressions and body language. Part of communicating is learning how to see what people are saying without using words. You can start by really learning how to read facial expressions. If you say something and the person takes a step back or leans back away from you and their eyes widen, it could mean you said something that shocked or offended them. If they nod, it means they agree with you. If their eyes lower to the floor, it could mean several things. You might have said something that reminds them of something that saddens them. Eyes cast down are sometimes indicative of shame.

Keeping Empathy Even When You are Upset with Someone

One of the most common complaints in interpersonal relationships is feeling like the other person does not listen to them and see their perspective. When we look at the other person's point of view, we can see how our words and actions affect them, and it might even change our time. At the very least, we will realize that there is more to the situation than we first thought.

Say, for example, your friend has not been responding to you lately and has broken commitments. It would be easy to become frustrated and assume that they are not valuing your friendship. However, there might be a reason they have been unavailable that has nothing to do with spiting you. Part of empathy is not assuming. Before you send a text marked with anger, try giving them a call. Tell them you're concerned about them and ask if there is something they need to talk about. You might find out that they have something going on in their life. Maybe they are struggling with financial issues. Perhaps their loved one is sick. If it is not their usual behavior to be unavailable, the reason behind it might have nothing to do with you. Worst comes to worst, and they are doing something to spite you; how much of a loss would that friendship be anyways?

More often than not, the things people do are not about us. This ties into the next point. Part of empathy is not taking things personally. It will not only be maddening for you to assume that the things other people do care about you, but it renders you unable to have empathy for them.

Do not hold people to such high standards. In the end, people are just people. They are not always on their game. Sometimes they will say things that come out the wrong way. You might have caught them at a bad time.

Forgiveness is part of empathy. Wouldn't it be great if we were always on top of our game and always spoke sweetly to each other? However, we don't live in that world. In the world we live in, people get tired, irritable. We have bad days, and our fuse is shorter than usual. We have miscommunications. Your friends and loved ones will need forgiveness from you, and you will need forgiveness from them.

It is essential not to forgive other people but to forgive yourself. To forgive another, you must forgive your reaction to them. Ignoring that, you give yourself the safety to move on. Let's say your loved one does something that genuinely hurts you. When they realize what they have done, it will hurt them to see that. Their shame is laid bare. They are now angry less at you than themselves. Forgive to be set free.

Free yourself the same way. You will develop an unhealthy mindset if you remind yourself of your past mistakes. If we had time machines that let us undo our mistakes, we would all get one, but that is impossible. If you are feeling bad, that energy will spread to the others in your life. Both positive and negative emotions are contagious. If you feel inner turmoil, those around you will sense it, and you will sense it.

How uncomfortable was it to be around them? You try to reassure them, but it will not work. They can't even stop self-punishing when it is time for someone else to be the focus.

Empathy for yourself is the beginning of having compassion for others. The harsh truth is that whatever you did not do in an instance in the past will never be done. What you did in the past will never change. What other people did in the past will never change. If you know deep down that you will not forgive the other person for their past transgressions towards you, do the best thing you can for everyone involved and distance yourself from them.

Your friends and your loved ones will never be perfect. If they have been in your life long enough, they have done things that did not sit well with you, and it will happen again in the future. Throughout our lives as humans, we will have bad days and react badly.

How to Apologize with Empathy

When we have arguments with someone, it is natural for our minds to gravitate towards our anger at them, how we cannot believe the things they said to us, words we wish we could've gotten in edgewise. That is because when our instinct to self-protect has taken hold of us.

We are only human, and therefore we will make mistakes in our lives and our relationships. There will be times that we have hurt the feelings of the people in our inner circle.

It is not easy admitting you have made a mistake and hurt someone. However, when you have, you cannot run from it. They will need to express the impact your actions had on them, and you will need to be willing to listen to what they have to say. Then you will need to apologize. People need to hear an apology from someone when they have hurt them. Just acknowledging what they have to say will make them feel like they have been heard and that their feelings have been validated.

It is essential to know how to give a proper apology.

- The best kind of apology is short and sweet. Try to avoid groveling or repeating yourself. It can make the person feel uncomfortable and cause a potentially freeing moment to feel heavy. Stick to the basics. Acknowledge what you did to them and that you realize you hurt their feelings.

- Say I know what I did was wrong, and you didn't deserve that. It shows that you care about the other person. It also shows that you are genuinely taking responsibility for what you have done. You are not blaming them, and you are not trying to minimize what you did.

●Once you have covered these essential basics, your sentence should be finished. There is one word you should never even consider using while giving an apology. The term "but" should be avoided entirely. Whenever you are giving your apology, temporarily delete the word "but" from your vocabulary. "I'm sorry, but…" is hurtful to hear. It is as if to say, "Now that I've gotten that out of the way, I can say what I want to say. Please do not bring up their part in the argument as a way to minimize your actions. It is also not the time to bring up personal woes to excuse yourself. An apology is a time to own up to your part of the transgression. Everyone argues, but with empathy, we fight for truth without the need to hurt the other person. We strive for a deeper understanding.

While it is essential to take responsibility for your actions, once you have apologized and been forgiven, it is done. It is time to let it go. If the other person does not let it go and continues to bring it up, this is abusive behavior. They are punishing you, and you can choose whether this is the behavior you want to put up with. It is advisable to distance yourself from this person if they're going to do the disciplinary action because it is unlikely they will stop and more likely that you will be subjected to more of it in the future.

Tips for Developing Empathy

Do you find it hard to feel empathy with other people? Is it hard for you to put yourself in someone else's shoes and feel what they are feeling?

Are the following statements factual for you?

- I don't understand how people can just let themselves think such terrible things about me.

- I get sick of just listening to them complain and being nothing but negative all the time.

- Why should I even bother? I can't change anything anyway. It would just be a waste of my time, and no one will ever care about me always.

- They don't even try to see things from my perspective.

- I feel like I am the only one who suffers in this world.

- I feel so alone and misunderstood.

- It is all a waste of time, they don't care about what I have to say, and they keep saying the same things over and over again; I can't believe people are so stupid.

If you relate to these statements, then chances are you have a hard time understanding others and their feelings, you find it hard to put yourself in someone else's place, you can quickly become withdrawn because of sadness or misery at home or in school, anxiety over social interactions and fear that you will be blamed for something.

Rebuilding Empathy

Empathy is the ability to understand another person, share their feelings and thoughts. It is the ability to "feel with" someone else by knowing that they have felt a certain way before and can still feel a certain way right now even though you are not next to him or her.

Different people have different empathetic abilities; some are better at gaining insight into others' emotions than others. Some people are predisposed to be compassionate or have more natural abilities, but either way, there is always room for improvement in this area of our life.

To build empathy, you can start by understanding your feelings and why you feel the way you do certain things.

Sometimes we cannot identify what triggers us, but something that happened in the past or has not happened yet would make it easier to empathize with others.

It helps, especially if you can identify what it was like for yourself and how it relates to someone else. It also helps to compare real-life situations in which you have been involved and have felt the same way others do. For instance, maybe a friend felt rejected by someone he admired, or perhaps he feels unwanted because people don't notice him when they are in his presence.

It also is beneficial to you if you can identify these feelings in yourself. Knowing about why you feel this way helps you gain insight into what it is like to be another person. It helps a lot and enables you to understand what they're going through.

If your classmate has a problem with a person that he or she likes and the person rejects them, then maybe looking at yourself in that situation would help because of the enormous amount of pressure he or she has to deal with. You may not be "the only one" that feels that way, but you probably know someone who is under the same pressure.

People are usually scared to talk about their feelings because they don't want to be judged or don't think anyone will understand them. Naturally, we would be afraid to reveal our vulnerabilities and fears in public because people will either form judgments or dismiss us as crazy or have an emotional disorder.

Experimenting with New Perspectives

You can try to put yourself in someone else's shoes if you think it will help you understand them better. For instance, let's say a friend feels sad and depressed because of something that people have said to her in the past. You can sit down with that friend and listen carefully to her feelings about what has happened to her and then ask her how she feels. She may feel stupid for feeling the way she does, or she may feel like everyone is horrible, but maybe after talking about it, you two find out that there are similar situations in which you have been involved.

If you feel like you understand her better because of this, you have gained something from her perspective. You have "been in that situation" and feel what she feels now that you are in it, whether or not it is the same situation. It can help you empathize with her more because there have been times that you were in her position.

Sometimes, a friend may be telling you about an upsetting incident at school that has happened to him or her, and it somehow relates to a specific issue at home. If nothing else, hearing about his or her feelings from his or her perspective can give him a better understanding and maybe get him out of his shell. You could help him sort things out by sounding out what he may be feeling and putting yourself in his position. For instance, maybe he feels like he is being punished for something that he did wrong, or perhaps it is not directly related to him, but it has a personal meaning for his family.

By focusing on listening carefully and asking questions, you can gain insight into someone else's feelings and emotions. You don't have to agree with them 100% of the time, but you have to try to see things from their perspective. You can use this as the basis for having an empathetic conversation with them and trying to understand what is going on inside their head.

You don't have to think about the people in the examples I gave you, but just think about how you would feel if those situations were happening to you. That is exactly how someone else that has been through that situation may feel. You now have understood someone else's feelings from a different perspective because of this experience that has happened to them.

It may seem far-fetched or silly at first, but it's essential to understand where other people are coming from because it helps us get over our problems or worries.

Empathy is the ability to fully understand others' states of mind, whether it is joy or pain. Let's deepen some aspects.

Additional Tips for Developing Empathy

1.Understand what "empathy" is. Empathy is the ability to understand and feel someone else's feelings as though they were your own. It doesn't mean that you feel sorry for them or pity them; instead, it means that you see things from their perspective and understand their feelings on an intense level.

2.Actively work on developing this skill. Reading this article and thinking about how you can build your empathy isn't cut it. If you want to make any progress, you're going to have actually to do something. This means:

3.You are putting yourself in other people's shoes. The first thing we need to do is learn how other people see the world through their own eyes and then step into their perception of the world for ourselves.

4.Empathize with people from all walks of life. If you only empathize with people who are just like you, or people who have things in common with you, then you're not going to be as good at it as you could be.

5.Similarity does indeed breed contempt; similarity also promotes empathy. Empathy grows when we are happier seeing the world as it is than seeing it from our perspective. So, when someone else has a similar life and similar experiences to yourself, your empathy for them is more significant than if they didn't share any of your experiences.

6.Focus on the similarities between yourself and other people, rather than the differences. It is because empathy develops more naturally when you can see other people as just like you. It's essential to focus on this similarity to build it up, but at the same time, make sure to remind yourself that there are differences.

7.Re-evaluate your life to find more things in common with others. Sometimes we can get trapped in our own lives and think that everyone else has an entirely different life from us — but this is rarely true.

8.Empathy is something we can actively cultivate in ourselves. It's not something that comes naturally; it takes work to develop, and the more we work at it, the better we get at being able to empathize with other people. If we want to be a better person, one of the first things we need to do is improve our empathy skills. Over time, as you develop these skills, they will become as easy as breathing — they'll just be second nature to you.

By working on your empathy skills, you can make tremendous progress in developing a better person's quality. It's not going to happen overnight; it'll take some time and effort, but if you set your mind to it, you'll start seeing significant improvements in your life very quickly. Start developing these skills today to become a better person tomorrow.

Now, I know that what I'm saying might sound confusing, especially if you need to see material results to register progress. However, evaluating yourself and accepting your flaws is a big step that you need to take.

Why is Empathy so Important in the Labor Market and Leader Training

The labor market is flooded with qualified candidates and vice versa. What sets a person apart from the competition? When assessing a potential employee, it's all about fit. An easy way to evaluate that is by taking their empathy levels into account when you interview them.

Empathy is a fundamental human trait, and it's crucial to the success of any business. Since empathy is so important, how can you increase your own and the empathy levels within your team members?

The answer to that question lies in superior leader training. Empathy has been known to be one of the primary skills taught in current employee training programs. Leaders can become more adept at reading their employees by using various empathy assessments and exercises.

Empathy can be increased through specific exercises offered by superior leader training methods. Not only can the heart be raised on a personal level, but it can also be implemented in a group setting.

One such way of increasing empathy is by being able to take another's perspective. It is offered as an exercise in many exceptional leader training programs. To perform this exercise, individuals are instructed to pair up with their peers and pick something specific to view from another's perspective. For instance, one person may focus on what it is like for the other person to have something referred to as multiple sclerosis, making everyday tasks such as opening doors difficult. The other person may focus on what it is like for the disease to have friends from school.

This exercise gets at the idea of perspective-taking through empathy. To take another's perspective, a leader must have compassion toward those they lead. One way to do this is through feedback. A leader can respond to their employees' work with empathy, but this can be not easy because many leaders tend to shield themselves rather than extend it toward others. It can make feedback difficult and even uncomfortable for employees receiving negative comments in their work reports; however, they must be given constructive criticism rather than taking it personally.

Empathy in both groups and individual settings can be improved through the use of specific exercises. Leaders can acknowledge their employees' strengths and weaknesses, which can lead to better communication and increased productivity. It allows leaders to make decisions using a broad perspective, which is critical when building a team.

Empathy is a fundamental human trait that is highly prized today in the workplace. As such, leaders of any type need to acknowledge, deliberate, and take others' perspectives when making decisions on behalf of their employees. Empathy-building exercises such as this help leaders better relate and grow as managers within their team.

Empathy is the ability to understand and share the feelings of another. It often manifests as having a sense of "knowing what another person is feeling without being told." The idea that empathy is essential in the labor market and leadership training has been around for decades, but it has been revised with modern-day research. Compassion has shown to have many benefits on both employers/leaders and employees/followers of a company or organization.

Empathy is crucial because it makes a good leader. Imagine if you were leading troops in battle. If you could empathize with the soldiers, would they be more willing to follow you into action? In reality, empathy can be useful in all types of situations. Not only is it beneficial on an individual level, but it also benefits the broader community. It is why we should value empathy in both employees and leaders.

Empathy is vital in leadership positions and employment opportunities because it can make a person more successful on both an individual and community-wide level. Empathy allows for effective communication with others and better decision-making skills. If a boss or leader is not empathetic, they may make mistakes that can affect the outcome of an entire organization or group. It includes not making effective decisions about hiring and promotions. Empathy is also essential because it makes leaders more successful. Consider the person who is applying for a job with your company. How will their interview go if they do not have empathy? They will probably be less likely to get the job.

Empathy has also shown to be essential for forming successful relationships within an organization's primary goal of creating customer satisfaction and building a business (Buckingham & Coffman, 2009). Leaders and followers need to work together to achieve these goals, so the relationship between leaders and their employees/followers is essential.

In the workplace, empathy is related to how employees learn from one another. When we are more empathetic about someone's situation, we often feel for that person and become willing to listen. By doing so, everyone benefits from a better chance at success.

How to Develop Empathy in Your Everyday Life?

Compassion is a word that is utilized regularly by numerous individuals. It's generally realized that sympathy is something to be thankful for, yet it isn't needed continuously in individuals' lives.

Did you realize that 98% of individuals can relate to other people? A couple of exceptional cases are insane people, narcissists, and sociopaths, who can't comprehend or identify with other individuals' sentiments and feelings.

Different gatherings of individuals that may battle understanding other individuals' feelings are the individuals who are on the Autism Spectrum. In any case, numerous individuals feel that individuals on the Autism Spectrum are as yet fit for identifying with other individuals' feelings, albeit maybe not in a conventional way.

While a vast, more significant part of the populace is equipped for sympathy, some of the time, its act is constrained. In any case, what is compassion, and for what reason is it significant?

Would empathy be created, or would we say we are brought into the world with a specific sum? Are a few people just naturally better at identifying? Is it truly as significant as specific individuals state it is to rehearse compassion? We should take a plunge.

A 'mind reader' will usually pick up or over-emphasize individual small signals and believe that other people dislike them or have negative thoughts. There are so many reasons why a person might be giving outbid vibes,' and most of the time, it probably isn't you. They could be tired, have a bad day, or perhaps one of their loved ones is terminally ill. Maybe they have a rash in an uncomfortable place, or maybe they are on a low ebb. You generally don't have the insight to tell which of these reasons are the right one, so you have to take your 'mind reading' perceptions with a pinch of salt.

When you recognize these thought patterns, you need to recognize them as irrational. That doesn't mean everything is peachy and that you ignore the flaws, but you have a grounded, rational perception of the situation. Maybe it's you, and perhaps it isn't. All you can do is approach the problem from a logical, calm perspective and carry on.

It is also worth mentioning that people who are curious and interested are also happier in a similar vein. Research on the exact reason why it is still in its nascent stages and several hypotheses are floating around. We know that people with higher intelligence tend to be more curious, so some people have theorized that intelligence is causally responsible for the increases in happiness. Several studies have documented that intelligence alone does not lead to more happiness than average, so it appears that curiosity is itself the key ingredient.

Another, perhaps more likely reason why curiosity is connected to happiness is that curiosity leads to opportunities. If something piques your interest, pursuing it might lead to a positive outcome. You might find a new hobby, make a meaningful relationship, advance your career or develop new interests.

It has also been used to explain the relationship to intelligence. Curiosity is stimulating. It makes us explore the unknown, and when you are not familiar with something, your brain has to work harder.

Chasing your interest puts you outside your comfort zone, and you don't know all the information and rules you need to succeed yet, so your mind has to find them out.

Of course, some of you may counter with the notion that curiosity is a trait. You can't learn to be curious any more than you can learn to be tall or handsome. Yet the research disagrees – positive psychology is arguing that curiosity is a habit that can be reinforced through deliberate effort.

So, how do you cultivate curiosity? By overcoming fear. Fear is the obstacle that keeps you from chasing those untraveled trails of your interest – fear of financial insecurity, fear of social embarrassment, fear of failure. Every time you have a slight curiosity, it's these nagging doubts and fears that stop you from walking the yellow brick road.

Ultimately, you have to let these fears go. It is a complex process, but its foundation relies on the idea that you don't need to control everything. If there is no risk of failure, then you are not trying anything new, and you are not feeding your curiosity. You need to go with the flow and let yourself enter novel situations. If you manage to do this, you can chase your interest, opening the door to new experiences.

Empathy is essential for jobs and leadership positions that require close interactions with others, but its importance goes beyond the professional sphere. Empathy training has a direct impact on our emotional well-being, which in turn affects physical health. Empathy should be at the top of any list of traits desirable in both a skilled practitioner as well as a good leader.

Well-Being

The World Health Organization (WHO) regards health as a vital part of one's life.

To be well with ourselves, we have to take care of all our life points, from the body to the most profound emotions. Well-being encompasses all the relational environments of our lives: family, work, friendships, neighborhood, communities.

If you are satisfied with your life, the chances are that you don't overthink what you should do to become better. Sure, you are working hard to get a promotion, you renovated your house a while back, and you even started taking care of your body. While all this can make you feel excellent and satisfied with who you are, they are not very important in the long run. It is important to develop yourself, find your inner peace, and allow others to see everything you have to give.

It can be challenging to do if you are alone, but discussing with a sincere friend can help you. Make sure that you emphasize from the beginning that no matter what you hear will offend you, you are making a change in your life, so it is expected to go through things that might upset you a little bit. Your friend only wants the best for you, so don't take it personally if you tell you that you need to be more honest or dedicated to your work.

Once you hear your flaws from their perspective, be honest to yourself and see if they are right; should you pay more attention to truth and lies? Are you procrastinating more often than you should? Writing the essential things that you want to change on a piece of paper will help you remember them and visualize the work that you have to do. Remember: these are no longer problems, so you shouldn't feel wrong about them. Positively look at them: these are things that will disappear to help you become better and better.

If you don't feel comfortable admitting your flaws in front of others, you can acknowledge them by thinking about the moments when you failed; why didn't it work out? If you had done something different, things would have been better? For example, your last relationship might have failed because your partner complained about you being dishonest. In this case, it is easily understood where the problem is and why you have to solve it.

All this seems depressing? It might be, but it is the first step towards improvement. You will feel worst before feeling better, but in the end, it all depends on the way you choose to look at this process: with positivity or negativity.

How Can You Get Better?

Simple problems have simple solutions, and once you realized what your issues are, you can write down small things that you can do to eliminate them. If one of your problems is procrastination, find a way to plan your time accordingly; give yourself one hour to relax and 20 minutes to work. It will be easier for you to follow the plan if you don't have to make significant changes suddenly.

Your Health is Suffering

Perhaps you are unable to feel the motivation to pursue your goals because you are ill, or you have been leading an unhealthy lifestyle that is finally starting to catch up to you. If you feel sluggish, tired, or have chronic pain, you could be experiencing these because of your lifestyle. If you have brain fog, which is the inability to focus, you could have lost your motivation due to your lifestyle. This one is a somewhat simple fix: consider adopting a healthier way of living. Look to change your diet, your exercise routine, or seek medical care.

The Goals that You Have Set are Too Small or Too Big

If you set goals that are too small, it will not inspire you to complete them; besides, creating too high or too big plans will make you feel like you do not have the confidence to accomplish them. To avoid this, make your goals reachable. Set the goals that allow you to achieve success, but make them just far enough to reach that you grow in the process. Prepare yourself up for success for you to feel good about yourself.

You are Impatient. One of the final reasons that you could be lacking the motivation to finish your goals because you simply think that you should have reached them by now. Impatience will cause you to quit often before you even start. You'll stop because you feel like it's taken too long to reach your goals. To combat this, you need to take pleasure in the journey and understand that the progress you are making will take time. As you accomplishing the small steps, consider rewarding yourself for your progress. When you acknowledge the progress you've made, it allows you to slow down and see that you accomplish something.

Tips for Succeeding

When you are setting your goals, you need to find out why you want to achieve them. What is going to be the force behind your motivation? As you are considering the power behind your inspiration, make sure that the reasons for pursuing a goal are strong enough. Also, make sure that the proper motivation is there. When you set small, weak goals, you are not giving yourself a chance to feel motivated by them. Consider what you will gain when you complete your goals and make sure to inspire you.

See Your Success. Visualization techniques are helpful, and you should use them when you can. Visualize yourself being successful and experience the emotions and the feeling that come along with that success. Also, visualize yourself feeling a failure. When you do this, allow yourself to handle all of the emotions that come along with failing. It is essential because it can motivate you to continue.

Support. It's a good idea to ensure that the environment you are in is supportive. The more rooting people, the better you will feel as you pursue your goals.

Perspective Matters. Consider changing your perspective on life. If you tend to look at life and see the positive things, motivation may not be an issue for you. However, if you look at life and tend to focus on the negative, try making a habit of looking for the good things life offers. They are there, and you have to look for them. Sometimes, they are small things such as a baby laughing or getting inside before it rains. Other times, they are big, and you will notice them. You were focusing on the positive rather than the negative will help you change your outlook on life.

Seek Out Help. Find motivation through others, such as a life coach, friends, or mentors. When you see someone successful and admire them, consider finding out their tips and secrets. More often than not, people will be happy to help you out. One day, when you get the chance, make sure that you help someone as well.

Go Big, Start Small. Get yourself going; make sure that your dreams are big but that you are starting small. No matter what it takes, be sure that you are getting started. As you go along the journey, take breaks and rest not to lose your momentum. Your goals are achievable, and you deserve to make them a reality.

Our emotions can either control us or help us. If we allow them to control us, we are harming ourselves and our relationships. When we allow our emotions to help us, we can learn to harness the power behind them. We feel the emotions can keep us from harm, spur on change, and manipulate our situations. By learning to harness the power behind them, we are using every resource available to us.

When we look at the emotions that run to our body, they can be intimidating and complicated. But when we know how to harness the power, we can gain success that we didn't know was possible.

Defining Self-Defeating Thoughts

When people happen to be depressed or anxious or low on self-esteem, they react to everything present around them. Under this condition, they develop the habit of overthinking almost everything present near them, be it something that concerns them or not. This habit of overthinking leads them to affirm the negative thoughts that shroud their rationality.

Once a negative thought challenges an individual who is already having a wrong time trying to fight depression or anxiety, he (or she) can do nothing besides bowing down to them. Such individuals bow down to these thoughts and reaffirm whatever negative opinions they have about themselves through these thoughts. They build upon the negative beliefs and contribute to their fears and support the already depleted self-esteem.

This distorted thinking has been distributed into numerous types by prominent psychologists. Psychologists call this style of thinking distorted thinking because you distort reality to look at things the way your mind wants you to. You're painting a gloomy picture of the things around you and the negativity around you so deludes you that you're not trying to counter the negative thoughts through the pervasive power of positive evaluations.

Realize Negative Events

Behind every negative thought you come across, there has to be an adverse event instigating that pattern. Just like we have studied so many times above, the negative thoughts encountered by you are doing to a particular type of thinking pattern that you have developed with time. You look for evidence to prove this thinking pattern and don't look for evidence other than that.

Now, when it comes to identifying the self-defeating thoughts you encounter, you need first to identify the events that cause such a reaction. If we go by the principles of cause and effect, every response in this world is caused by past action before it. The reaction that you are undergoing is a doing of an event that you have encountered.

What made you feel that you aren't good for this world and are unlovable? What made you host this particular perception? What was that specific feeling that got you thinking in this manner? Was it a message from an ex-friend? Was it something nice that someone did to you? Or was it because you started comparing yourself to others?

You must realize what makes you go down deep into the world of wonderland and distorted thinking exactly. The things influencing your negative thoughts need to be cleared, and you need to view them without any obstructions whatsoever. Only when you identify what exactly is pushing you through the negativity, you can help spot where the problems lie.

For instance, most people go towards distorted thinking when they consider themselves guilty about a possible solution. Your team at work wasn't able to achieve its objectives; you had a wrong thought about the relationship that just ended or had a lousy time comparing your family to others. All of these thoughts can make you feel guilty about possible outcomes. You then go for the easy way out and start thinking negatively. You have been conditioned to think negatively, which is why no other option can spring up in your mind.

Constant Practices to Achieve Personal Well-Being

All of us want to be happy. No matter what goal or activity we are currently working towards, in the end, we are just seeking contentment, happiness, and inner peace. Yet, above all other qualities, happiness is elusive. Most of us are just aimlessly wandering around, hoping we trip upon satisfaction below our feet.

Research on positive psychology is still in its infancy, with most of the initial efforts in psychology to treat illness and mental disease. However, scientists are starting to recognize the overwhelming importance of taking an active effort to improve your mental well-being, making the steps towards happiness elucidated.

Mindfulness

Mindfulness is quickly becoming the next fad. Lifestyle magazines, blog posts, and popular psychology articles mention mindfulness as a cure for many of our problems but skim over why. We will look at both how mindfulness helps improve happiness and the myriad of ways you can include mindfulness into your lifestyle.

So, what's the deal with mindfulness? Why try to be aware of our feelings and sensations all the time? Well, to start with, mindfulness helps you avoid negative and intrusive thoughts. It has been documented that people who daydream are less happy than their mindfulness peers. Our current understanding of this phenomenon is simply that mindfulness quietens all those difficult thoughts that you usually brood upon; I need to lose weight, I don't want to go to work on Monday, I hate my job (and so on). Instead, mindfulness makes you focus on the here and now. You cut out all that negativity and just simply be. It doesn't mean mindful people don't tackle their problems; they just meditate and worry less.

Sleep

One of the weirdest parts of modern society is the fact that we celebrate our lack of sleep. Yet we can't. Rest is beyond crucial to our physical and mental well-being, with a legion of horrible consequences if we ignore our tiredness.

For example, a lack of sleep can cause you to put on weight. Sleep affects how our body releases insulin, affecting how our body reacts to glucose and how many calories we retain from our diet.

Of course, sleep deprivation is also associated with numerous psychological side effects too. People who don't get enough sleep have more inadequate concentration than their well-rested peers, and they also struggle to form and access long-term memory. Chronic sleep deprivation is known to cause and contribute to depression, anxiety, and stress. When you digest the host of physical and mental problems a lack of sleep causes, it is blindingly obvious that a good sleep routine is vital to our overall happiness and well-being.

People often face the problem when they try to improve their sleep habits because they try too hard. It sounds counter-intuitive, but worrying and stressing about your lack of sleep is believed to be a potential cause of insomnia.

Owing to this, the best ways to improve your sleeping patterns tend to be related to sleep hygiene and lifestyle. It includes making an effort to ensure the following:

- Make your sleeping space is as dark as possible, which includes turning all electronic devices off and potentially buying thicker, darker curtains.

- Avoid artificial lighting before you go to sleep, especially lighting from computer devices. Consider purchasing white or natural lighting for your bedroom.

- Have a regular sleeping routine; wake up and go to bed at the same time every day.

- That you are not too hot or cold; use lighter or heavier duvets and sheets and open or close windows to get the right temperature.

- In addition to this, it's useful to expose yourself to natural light. Our body changes our sleeping habits according to the presence of natural light, which is why we tend to feel more tired in winter when it is darker during the days. Taking 5-10 minutes in the morning to sit by a window and let the sun radiate over your body is a great way to tell your body clock that you should be awake at that time.

- Finally, you should also cut out the caffeine. It's an obvious tip but essential to state nonetheless. The stimulating effects of caffeine can take up to 6 hours for your metabolism to deal with, which is increased if caffeine is already in your system. It often leads to a caffeine build-up in coffee and soft-drink addicts, with their bodies needing several days for all the caffeine in their approach to be expunged. Yes, it's challenging to drop the caffeine habit, and you will probably feel awful as your body adjusts. Yet it's necessary – caffeine fixes your tiredness but ruins your sleep, which causes you to be tired. It's a trap, and you know it. Cut it out.

Practice Gratitude

Grateful people are also happier, or so the evidence suggests. It might garner the apparent response that perhaps appreciative people have more cause to be thankful than the average person – that they are wealthier, more attractive, and overall, more successful. The evidence paints a different picture, claiming that gratitude is mostly independent of other socio-economic factors and can be practiced without any exceptional circumstances.

So why does gratitude seem to be one of the most prominent contributors to happiness? Psychologists are still investigating, and numerous hypotheses are being put forward. One train of thought suggests that being grateful makes you savor your life experiences more, which in turn causes two other psychological changes. The first is a greater sense of satisfaction, but the second is that you actively seek out and embrace more life experiences, leading to more reward and pleasure.

Gratitude also seems to benefit your self-esteem and confidence positively. Many of us suffer psychologically from not feeling loved or appreciated, even when supportive friends and family surround us.

Taking a few moments to feel grateful for other people's actions makes you more receptive and welcoming of all the love and friendship other people provide. It not only makes you more empathetic and self-compassionate, but gives you a sense of your value. After all, if people are willing to do things for you, you must mean something to someone.

Smiling

It is especially intriguing that humans can produce and distinguish between a genuine smile and a fake smile. The folk wisdom that a genuine smile originates from the eyes rings true, as the facial muscles around the eye cannot be explicitly controlled. Therefore, when we fake a smile, only the mouth and cheek move, which we recognize as forced.

Nonetheless, even forced smiles appear to have an impact on how we feel. It has been discovered that other facial expressions also impact our bodies and our brain, with fake fearful words producing a higher heartbeat and a rise in body temperature, even without the corresponding emotion.

However, this doesn't mean you can smile all your troubles away. If you have a strong negative feeling, such as sadness or frustration, smiling won't magically make your feelings dissipate. Nonetheless, if you are in an emotional void or neutral state, letting out a fake smile might nudge you towards feeling a little more upbeat and relaxed.

With that being said, be careful with your fake smiles! Smiling at inappropriate times will get you a negative response from the people around you, which won't improve your happiness (I.e., don't smile when someone tells you they are in pain). We all have encountered people who smile when they feel angry or stressed in social situations, and as you might know, the result is very uncomfortable for everyone around.

The exact mechanism through which smiling makes you feel happier isn't understood. One theory suggests that altering blood flow to your face during a smile directs less blood to your brain, which gives you a small 'happy' sensation. Alternatively, we likely have some inbuilt feedback loop between our expressions and our mood. For example, people who adopt confident, relaxed postures experience a release of hormones, making them feel more confident. Therefore, the same might be right for other emotions and expressions (such as fear expression leading to a rise in core body temperature).

Exercise

We all know exercise is okay – just about every self-help advice we have ever read or listened to has wisely recommended a workout now and then. Yet, just how effective is an exercise to our long-term mental well-being and happiness?

It has been theorized that exercise tackles and manages the physical aspects of stress, anxiety, and depression. When we exercise, the hormones and neurotransmitters released help control and alleviated the physical strains of exercise – shortness of breath, constricted blood flow, bodily pain. Yet, these are often related to or symptoms of mental health issues. Therefore, by hitting the gym, you can tackle some of the cognitive problems you may have, but through the body.

Yet, the effects of exercise also seem to go above and beyond this. Movement appears to improve neural plasticity and neurogenesis, which is your brains' ability to learn new things and your brains' ability to grow and foster new cells. As people get older, neural plasticity decreases, and that children are better at picking up further information and learning than older people. Likewise, as we get older, our brains tend to shrink, which is why the elderly tend to have more insufficient memory and slower cognition than their younger peers.

When we perform aerobic exercise, neurogenesis takes place in the hippocampus – the area of the brain responsible for learning and long-term memory. The exact cause of this is not fully understood. However, the working hypothesis involves releasing the protein BDNF (brain-derived neurotrophic factor), which doesn't just help new neurons grow. Still, it actively protects older neurons from loss of plasticity and repairs damaged neurons.

Help Others

People who engage in helpful behaviors to other people tend to be happier than people who don't. Charity workers, volunteers, community leaders, and even people who do small, spontaneous acts of helpfulness all seem to be happier than your average Joe. It was initially thought that more comfortable people were more inclined to help others (which still appears to be confirmed). However, it is also understood that there is a causal relationship between giving people a helping hand and your state of mind.

As with most phenomena on happiness, there is a tremendous amount of research and study on-going, examining why this relationship exists. Our current understanding believes that helping others improves your state of mind for several reasons. To start with, giving to other people just feels nice. Some philosophy strains have argued that nearly all altruistic behavior is only for your benefit – by making us feel better.

Yet there is a lot more to be helpful than the so-called 'helpers high.' By giving our aid and effort to others, we also provide ourselves with purpose and life satisfaction. Many people feel lost, drifting through their lives without a goal or a target to motivate them to carry on. In this situation, taking the initiative to help others can guide light to give life meaning.

Even for more motivated individuals, achieving goals by helping others seems to boost your feeling of confidence and self-worth. People who meet goals generally feel more competent, able, and grounded than people who don't.

The Impact of Happiness on Physical and Mental Health

The impact of happiness on physical and mental health is massive, maybe even more than you think. It's time to stop being ashamed or embarrassed by the word "happy" and get to know all about how it affects your body, brain, mood, and sleep.

Health and happiness go hand in hand. If you're healthy, chances are you're also feeling pretty decent about your life right now. And if you feel good, chances are it's easier for you to take care of your health and well-being. But what is the impact of happiness on physical and mental health?

Research has shown that a positive attitude is connected to physical health. Several studies have revealed that a happy person is generally more likely to stay healthy than someone who's not feeling cheerful. These studies can even predict a person's chances of developing certain medical conditions like heart disease or cancer.

In one study, Dr. Andrew Steptoe, from University College London (UCL), found that a positive attitude can help people live longer lives. The results of his research showed that the most common characteristic of an optimistic person was the ability to bounce back from stress or trauma quickly. If you can handle adverse situations with ease, you'll likely be able to avoid certain diseases and infections.

A happy person is generally more likely to stay healthy than someone who's not feeling so cheerful.

Ways that Happiness Positively Affects Your Physical Health

1.Happiness improves circulation, which reduces inflammation in your body and builds tissue.

2.Happy people have less cholesterol in their blood, decreasing their risk of developing heart disease or a stroke.

3.A happier outlook can impair the progression of Alzheimer's disease.

4.Happiness reduces stress, which is the number one cause of heart disease.

5.Happy people live longer.

6.Happy people have more robust immune systems and produce more of the protective cells T cells.

7.Happy people are less likely to have a stroke.

8.Happy people are less likely to die from cancer or accidents; not only does happiness improve your fitness level, but it improves your mental preparation for any physical competition you may be involved in (think ball hockey, basketball, tennis, etc.).

9.Happy people recover from colds faster than unhappy people.

10.Happy people get higher grades in school, translating into better jobs and higher earning potential later in life.

Ways that Happiness Affects Other People You Care About

1.Happy people live healthier lives and tend to have less disease or difficulties with aging.

2.Happy people have more energy, which translates into physically stronger kids who are more likely to excel in sports.

3.Happy people leave a better impression on friends and family than unhappy persons, giving them more influence on their loved ones and more respect from others.

4.Happy people have a better sense of humor, making them more fun to hang around, resulting in more people wanting to spend time with them.

5.Happier people make fewer mistakes in their careers, giving them more promotion and advancement opportunities, thus a higher earning potential.

Ways that Happiness Impacts Your Mental Health

1.Happiness is your body's natural drug.

2.You can wake up feeling happy, even if you don't have a good night's sleep.

3.Happy people can recover from work stress more quickly than unhappy people.

4.Happy people are more creative, experienced, and in control of their thoughts and feelings.

5.Happy people enjoy the moment and are less likely to worry about things they cannot control.

6.Happy people have sharper memories plus better short-term and long-term recall, which translates into better grades in school (and a higher earning potential later in life).

7.Happy people are more outgoing and tend to have more same-sex friends.

8.Happy people are more trustworthy and have a giant circle of friends.

9.Happier people like themselves better, and depression is less likely to set in overtime.

10.Happier people have better leadership qualities that can influence their team members to perform better.

And to top it all off, happier people live longer in general.

6.Happy people are more likely to be promoted than unhappy people at work.

7.Happy parents have happier children.

8.Happy spouses leave better impressions on friends, which gives the person who is happy a broader social circle. The happy person's spouse receives more positive attention (which can boost self-confidence when they see how much others admire their spouse).

Ways that Happiness Affects Your Sleep

1.Happiness is soothing and relaxing, making a person less likely to toss and turn when they cannot sleep.

2.Happy people produce more melatonin, which is the hormone that regulates your sleep cycle.

3.Happier people are more likely to seek a natural remedy for their insomnia, giving them a better quality of relaxation than taking sleeping pills.

4.Happy people tend to have regular sleep patterns, making them easier to predict when it comes time for bed.

5.Happy people are often better problem solvers when they get into trouble and need to sleep.

6. Happy people feel more comfortable in their beds.

7. A happier mood can reduce the amount of time it takes you to fall asleep.

8. A happy outlook makes it easier to sleep after listening to some soft music.

9. A happy upbringing tends to make children more comfortable for parents to put down at night (meaning that they will sleep better).

10. A happy and supportive relationship (with a happy partner) is also helpful for falling asleep.

Ways that Happiness Affects Your Immune System

1.Happy people produce more T cells, which are necessary for long-term immune health.

2.Happy people have more positive interactions with their friends and family, translating into protection of their immune system.

3.Happy people get more sunlight (which is the natural way to get vitamin D).

4.Happy people tend to eat healthier foods, meaning they can fight off sickness easier than unhappy persons.

5.Happy people tend to be more physically active, which helps increase their immune systems.

6.Happy people leave a better impression on others, giving them a broader social circle and more protection against illness.

7.Happier relationships (with a happy partner) give the person who is happy a better defense against disease.

8.Happy parents spend more time with their children, which gives the children an immunity boost. Happier parents are also more likely to keep the kids healthier by providing healthier food and keeping them away from sick people.

9. The brain is an immune organ, meaning that happiness can help boost your body's natural defenses to fight disease, infection, and illness.

10.Stress can kill us, so if you are stressed out or unhappy, it can harm your immune system.

Stress is one of the most common causes of doctor visits. Any number of factors can cause it, but there are various approaches to managing stress. The best method to managing stress is to learn how to relate to it and let it go.

The way we relate to our emotions is through our beliefs, thoughts, and behaviors. When we believe something (such as that our job is a waste of time) or feel an emotion (such as anger), these are things that we can learn to accept.

When we try to suppress or ignore our emotions, we simply make them worse. To successfully manage stress, you must learn how to control your moods, not repress them.

While it can be difficult for us humans to do, learning how to improve our health through happiness is not only attainable but inevitable.

Most people know that good health depends on a positive mental attitude, but it doesn't stop there. Positive emotional health also affects physical health. Happiness improves physical and psychological health by increasing circulation and reducing stress hormones. Regular aerobic exercise can help with your state of mind as well.

If you are struggling to find an answer to your sleep problems, here is a great article that will walk you through the process of improving sleep.

And on the topic of sleep, here is a great article that will walk you through the process of improving sleep.

With all this being said in mind, remember, happy people tend to be healthier and more comfortable, and happier people usually pay more attention to their health and overall life because they are more nutritious. If we choose happiness as our goal, we must select healthy habits to achieve our goals. It's a twofold concept that goes hand in hand. You can't have one or the other, and it's both. You can't increase your happiness by being unhealthy and expecting to last for long. If you want to be healthy, you will need to have happiness, positive emotions, and good relationships. These are the critical elements for long and healthy life.

The concept of healthy relationships is fundamental when it comes to overall health. Often, we don't see our connections with others as something that impacts our overall health, but they play an essential role in creating our health or lack thereof. If you are having a hard time, stay positive and focused on your health goal. If you are happy, then you will have a better chance to succeed.

One of the best things we can do for our bodies is to eat healthy food. It means choosing foods that are good for us and don't contain unhealthy ingredients like bacon, sugar, and unhealthy oils.

When it comes down to it, our bodies run on nutrients. It means ingesting foods that contain vitamins and minerals that our body needs to be healthy. It is good to get some exercise at least two or three times per week because it boosts the immune system and improves brain function. The best time to get in a workout is right after you wake up in the morning and before you go to bed at night.

It is essential to be careful with your diet and exercise as it can result in a loss of weight too fast or even lead to serious health problems. Make sure that you consult your doctor if you have questions about what is right for your body.

When it comes to finding time to get some exercise, walking is the best way to do it. It is a way that anyone can do and burn calories and the fat in the body. Investing in a treadmill (for example) can help get more exercise during the day.

Stay focused and enjoy yourself throughout this process of self-development! Good luck on your journey of success with these tips!

Are People Born with Empathy or Can it be Taught?

If you have empathy, it's always been there.

People are born with a natural capacity for empathy, but it is not always utilized. Some of the things that can inhibit empathy include lack of eye contact, emotional exhaustion, conflict with someone else's emotion or goal, and being overstimulated already. So, no matter what your disposition might be towards someone else's suffering—whether it be blind rage or an indifferent shrug—empathy is a resource that needs to be nurtured to grow into something more meaningful and lasting than just average everyday kindness. To do this, we need to practice compassion together while building resiliency and self-compassion within ourselves.

It is thought to be an acquired skill, not one that can be genetic because it requires experience in social interaction and communication.

Some researchers argue that people are born with an essential ability to feel what others feel, but these people are not born with the skills necessary to display empathy.

But research has found some evidence of compassion and empathy being related more deeply than just an acquired trait; they seem to come from a universal sense of morality rooted deep within all humans, or what some call "moral intuition." This moral intuition seems to naturally lead people into showing feelings for others' pain and discomfort.

Regina Sullivan, a neuroscientist at the University of Wisconsin-Madison, has done experiments using fMRI technology to study humans' and monkeys' brains.

In her research, she shows videos of people getting hurt by the subjects. She observes their reactions as they view these videos.

Her results show that feeling pain in certain parts of the brain, such as in areas related to empathy, predicts how much distress someone feels when watching another person suffer. Sullivan's research has helped us discover similarities between an infant's brain and an adult's brain when reacting to emotional situations. The more similar they are, the more alike their responses will be in feeling empathy and experiencing events such as pain.

One area in the brain that seems crucial in understanding what someone else is thinking or feeling is a brain region called the insula. This region becomes active when we are experiencing our pain and also when we are observing someone else's pain as well (Graziano, 2009).

In one experiment, researchers showed subjects videos of people getting needles stuck into them. This study found that the insula lit up in both the person being pricked and the person watching it. It suggests some hardwiring for empathy and that all humans have a certain level of empathic response wired into their brains (Harmon-Jones et al., 2012).

However, these results may be too little evidence to prove that all people are born with empathy.

In recent research, Marta Graziano, a psychology researcher at the University of California in Los Angeles, found that empathic responses may not be truly universal.

Graziano's group's study showed that when we feel empathy for someone else being hurt or hurting themselves, it is more likely if we have good personal relationships with them and if we spend a lot of time around them. It means that close relationships can teach us about other people's pain and distress, which is an acquired emotion rather than something innate (Graziano et al., 2013)."When we watch someone we know to suffer, or even imagine the pain they may be feeling, our brains react in a very similar way to reality," Graziano said (Graziano et al., 2013).

The concept of the empathic brain is similar to that of mirror neurons. These neurons can be either excitatory or inhibitory and are thought to influence how we relate to other people. When people experience another person's pain, they also feel pain in some regions of their brains. It suggests that empathy is an innate response because it makes us feel a connection with those around us and helps us develop different relationships with them (Graziano et al., 2013).

The development of empathy has been studied through various models. These models explore the stages of development during which the heart is either absent or is present. The literature assessments have been carried out to provide a comprehensive overview of these models to consolidate the current knowledge pertaining to the development of empathy in humans and other primates and its effect on prosocial behaviors.

One model that was proposed by Sternberg (1985) is that one's ability to practice empathy develops through stages of alternating inhibition and enhancement: initially, one is unable to inhibit emotional responses to others; but later, one learns how to deter them during certain situations but then become capable of feeling more intensely (e.g., when angry).

It's important to note that empathy isn't something we are born with a limited amount of, like just the ability to count to ten or read. Empathy is a capacity, something that can always be cultivated through use or development.

Being able to identify with other people who are experiencing similar emotions, even when you might not understand precisely what they're going through, is what makes us human. It also makes us compassionate towards them. We can also express this by being kind and caring towards people around us because of their emotional expressions or understanding of how they feel. It allows us a greater capacity for learning and compassion over time and helps make us more empathic.

According to Ian Maitland, a psychology professor at the University of Pittsburgh, "when individuals learn how to understand and recognize the emotions of others, they can attend more effectively to their needs. It is also known as empathic concern and can be characterized by more effective caretaking behavior (Matsumoto & Weisz, 2010)."

The tools necessary for this practice come from four different areas: education, emotional awareness, cognitive empathy, and experiential empathy.

The four tools include: identifying your feelings, understanding others' feelings and behaviors, learning about emotional cues, and developing appropriate responses.

Understanding and identifying our feelings is a vital part of the process of cultivating empathy. When we have a better experience of ourselves, we're able to better relate to others.

The next step is learning about emotional cues from others. Whether it's facial expressions, body language, or what their voice sounds like if they express sadness or frustration, the quickest way to understand someone else's feelings is by understanding ours. Understanding how someone else feels will allow us to know what they want by being more empathic.

Another essential tool in the empathy toolbox is listening for emotions expressed in those around us, even if we don't know exactly what those emotions might be.

The last part of the process is experiential empathy, which puts us in someone else's shoes, experiencing what they are experiencing and understanding it from their perspective. It can be facilitated by role-playing, guided meditation, or other creative methods to help us get out of our way and experience something new.

Experiential empathy allows us to develop more accurate and useful responses based on a foundation of understanding. It will enable us to de-escalate volatile situations or even improve emotional neglect in our personal lives.

We can also develop empathy by creating an empathetic response to any situation based on our ability to recognize and understand what we are feeling. Emotional intelligence is the ability to perceive and express emotion accurately and appropriately, make sound judgments and decisions, facilitate personal growth, and handle relationships effectively. Emotional intelligence includes:

Empathic relationships are characterized by compassion, understanding, concern, love, and a sense of connection between two people.

The key to creating this kind of connection is through the understanding of each other's experiences.

When we have this understanding, we can establish relationships with one another based on mutual trust.

The process of understanding the needs of others and providing for those needs is called caregiving. Caregiving can be done by teaching, listening, or sharing experiences. Each of these contributes to a relationship that is based on a foundation of trust.

Once this foundation is established, it allows people in empathic relationships to become closer and more connected emotionally because they feel like they're being understood. They have someone they can rely on when times are hard. The more empathy there is between two people, the more likely the relationship will last. An empathetic response can happen instantly, but it also takes time to develop into something more meaningful and lasting than average everyday kindness. For that to happen, we need to practice compassion together while building resiliency and self-compassion within ourselves.

Developing empathy is a skill that needs to be nurtured for it to grow into something meaningful and to last, like more effective caregiving behavior (Matsumoto & Weisz, 2010).

The four tools include: practicing open-ended, positive emotive behaviors (Ei & Maitland, 2016), practicing mindfulness meditation (Slagter et al., 2010), developing the capacity for compassion for yourself and others (Dalai Lama & Fritjof Capra, 1999), and learning more about what your emotional cues are telling you when you need some support.

The key to cultivating empathy is understanding that there is a difference between empathy and sympathy. Sympathy can be defined as feeling bad for a person who is suffering. Empathy can be defined as the experience of someone else's hurt or suffering.

There are also four different levels of empathizing with people.

While there is some proof that the capacity to relate followed to hereditary inclination, it's additionally evident that sympathy is an expertise that can be expanded or diminished.

One of the best ways for somebody to become empathic is for them to be prepared as kids. Compassion is a piece of instruction known as "enthusiastic insight." Teaching kids to think about how other individuals feel is a decent method for helping them create sympathy.

If a youngster harms another kid or prods them, it's useful to ask the kid how they think they made the other feel. You can ask them how they would feel on the off chance that somebody had treated them that way. Might they want to be prodded or harmed? Would they be dismal or angry on the off chance that somebody had treated them inadequately?

This line of thought can likewise be utilized for positive things. For instance, sharing is a significant piece of a small kid's instruction. Youngsters are frequently educated to share since they like it when others share it with them. It's anything but challenging to instruct kids to treat others with graciousness since they also might want to be dealt with sympathetic.

Discover Your Strengths

Everyone has talents, but not all of us use them. However, it's been found that people who don't exploit their abilities are less happy than their peers. Using your strengths is a two-part process; you have first to recognize what you are good at and then seek avenues to use this to your benefit.

To start with, search through your memories to periods in your life where you have been successful. What allowed you to be successful in that situation? What skills were you using? If you scour your past carefully, you will start to notice patterns and recognize your unique abilities. You must do this sincerely, however, even if you know where your strengths may lie. You might surprise yourself and recognize talents that you have failed to acknowledge or been misinterpreting your abilities.

If nothing comes to mind, you are doing it wrong. Consider the following talents;

- Athletic ability

- Critical thinking

- Teamwork

- Leadership

- Negotiation skills

- Problem-solving

- Dexterity

- Writing style & tone

- Public speaking skills

- Memory

One of the critical mistakes people make is that thinking talents need to be in a specific discipline, such as cooking or sports, or academia. Skills are often more subtle and transferable, which is why you need to take a little time to think about what singles you out.

Once you have recognized your strengths and talents, it's time to start making them a crucial part of your life.

It will be a slow journey – it isn't as simple as walking into a dream job and everyone recognizing how awesome you are. Start small – if you have writing talents, try your hand at writing recreationally in your spare time. Perhaps once you have built up a small repertoire of work, you can try your hand at writing for a small organization or company voluntarily. Later, you can start to look for paid employment, freelancing, and eventually into a full-time job where you are using your talents.

Self-Love Activities to Make You Love Yourself More

If you feel down about yourself, it doesn't have to be difficult to feel better. Self-love is easy with these self-care activities that will make you love yourself more. Self-care is often seen as a selfish activity, but it's actually beneficial for your well-being. You can use these activities as part of your self-love routine or give them as a gift to someone else who needs some support. Check out the self-love activities below and make sure to pick out one of your favorites!

1.Go for a long walk outside in nature – This will not only help you get fresh air and sunlight, but also look at nature's beauty.

2.Talk to a caring friend – A positive friend will help you feel better about yourself.

3.Watch a comedy or feel-good movie – Laughter is truly the best medicine. Try to watch funny movies, read a funny book, or try your hand at improve. You'll laugh and feel better about yourself.

4.Treat yourself to your favorite food – You do not have to eat junk food all the time. Sometimes, treat yourself to a healthy snack or a piece of your favorite cake!

5.Go online and look up things you love – Whether it's quotes, photos of people who inspire you, or books that you love, this is a great way to show yourself some love.

6.Write down three positive things about yourself – This is a great way to remind yourself of your positive traits and strengths. Try writing them down on sticky notes and putting them around your house. Alternatively, create an affirmation list for yourself! Post it somewhere where you can read it daily.

7.Buy yourself some flowers – Flowers are an easy way to make someone feel special and loved. They're also beautiful to look at. Put them somewhere where they can add some color to your space.

8.Create an affirmation list for yourself – Write down positive things that you want to tell yourself daily. Read these affirmations out loud every day at least once or twice, where there is no one else around.

9.Take a bath - A long bath with a favorite book or a nice candle is perfect for relaxing from the hustle and bustle of the world.

10.Get dressed up and do something fun – Try taking your favorite outfit out for a spin. Wear it once or twice a month and get some exercise, too.

11.Donate clothing or give the items to needy people – You don't have to wear everything you own, so why not go through your closet and donate clothes that you would just never wear? Go through your closets and donate anything that is outdated or no longer fits you well. Do the same with old toys and games, which are great for kids but not always exciting for adults. You can also give your clothing to poor people who need it more than you do.

12. Let someone you know feel special – Whether it's your mother, sister, girlfriend, or friend, be the one to help them feel special by buying them something meaningful or doing something nice for them.

13. Try an art project – Using items around the house, like paintbrushes or clay, can be incredibly therapeutic. It's also a great way to make sure you're using your time productively and not procrastinating on anything. Consider making art out of old magazines or other paper-based media.

14. Cut your hair – If you have been thinking about cutting your hair, now is a great time to do it! It can also be a great way to look and feel completely different. Consider changing up your hairstyle or color too!

15. Go to the library or bookstore and pick up a new book – There are so many ways you can learn more about yourself. Whether it's reading a self-help book, talking to friends, or doing something fun, self-improvement is an important part of self-love.

16. Read a funny book – This one is self-explanatory and will make you laugh. Reading something funny and funny books can help relieve stress.

17. Clean your room - There's nothing more fulfilling than going through your room and making it completely clean.

You'll feel much better knowing that all the clutter is gone, plus it'll look nice when you're done. If you don't want to spend too much time cleaning, at least put away some of your old clothes to see if you really like them and if they still fit you well.

18. Handwrite letters to friends or family — It's a nice way to show someone you care by actually writing them a letter. It can also be a great exercise in self-improvement to be able to write legibly!

19. Join a book club — Reading is a great way to learn about yourself, gain knowledge about things you're interested in, and have fun with friends. Consider reading a new book or experimenting with different types of books. Join a book club and decide as a group what you want to read each month.

20. Get lost in social media — You can relax with some of your hobbies or just check in on social media when you're bored or stressed out. Social media has so many benefits, like connecting with friends or learning new things that are valuable to your life.

21. Try a new hobby — If you're finding yourself constantly bored, try out a new hobby. This could be something as simple as cooking new recipes or learning to play a musical instrument.

22. Go for a bike ride — Biking to work or by yourself can be something fun and relaxing. You can make it part of your daily routine, or just do it when you feel down and lonely.

23.Start an exercise program - Doing something for yourself is important. It's not always easy to motivate yourself to get started, but starting an exercise program is helpful in both improving your mood and feeling better in general.

24.Take a nap – A 20-minute nap can have the same effect as a couple of hours of sleep. Try it out and see if it improves your mood.

25.Listen to upbeat music – Music is one of the best things to do for your mood. Many people have their favorite albums or playlists that they listen to when they're feeling down. You can also try something new, like upbeat pop music. This article has some recommendations for happy music that you can try out: 40 Happy Songs That Will Instantly Make You Feel Better

26.Watch your favorite TV show/movie – When you're feeling down, watching your favorite TV show or movie can be the perfect activity to unwind and relax. It's also a way to feel comforted while still doing something productive. Another thing you can do is watch a movie or TV show on Netflix and just let it play in the background as you surf the web or write an email. Just make sure that your favorite show doesn't have any dark moments (and that you don't take it literally to heart, like, if a character dies on screen, it would be better if you didn't go out and cry for three days).

27.Remember how much you love yourself – When things get tough and you start to question your worth, remember that life is about being happy and doing things that make us happy.

Don't forget that no matter what kind of day or week you've had, there are plenty of things that make up the whole picture.

28.Make a list of people who you think are completely amazing – These are not people who might have some flaws – these are the people who have done nothing but inspire you and make you work harder every day. You can make a list of their names on a piece of paper and keep it in your wallet. Then, when you feel down, just pull out the list to read through it.

Conclusion

People who have accepted the gift of loving themselves by making a firm commitment to do so have tremendous success in their lives. When you love yourself, you experience all of the advantages of higher self-esteem and confidence. People who love themselves aren't afraid to go the extra mile to reach the gold because they feel they deserve it. If you believe you are capable and trust yourself, you can do anything you want to do with your life. A significant part of being successful goes to people who believe that they can. Those who do not give up on themselves still will have failures and setbacks along the way to success, but they will not allow those accidental circumstances to stop them in their quest for the summit.

When you feel worthy of the best in life, you are more likely to attain it. Going after success because you think excellent has the power to transform your life totally and even can affect the lives of those you love and interact with.

When you are fully able to exercise self-love, you can pass it on to others. Learning the lessons of self-love will give you an aura of positivity reflected in the atmosphere wherever you are—passing it on means reinforcing other people by saying kind things to them, treating them fairly, and being encouraging and motivational whenever possible. Not only can you influence friends, neighbors, coworkers, and even strangers to treat themselves with reverence, but you can pass it on to your children.

Not surprisingly, if you lack self-love and compassion, it is likely that your parents or other relatives in your family experienced the same issue. Fortunately, you do not have to pass it on to the generations that come after you.

Empathy will make you feel better about yourself. But the real result of developing your empathic capacity will be the positive transformation in your emotional, social and work relationships.

Never forget to be yourself. Be realistic, optimistic and enjoy your life with joy and love.